# THE NIGHT
# ABRAHAM CALLED
# TO THE STARS

# THE NIGHT
# ABRAHAM CALLED
# TO THE STARS

poems

*Robert Bly*

Perennial

*An Imprint of* HarperCollins*Publishers*

A hardcover edition of this book was published in 2001 by HarperCollins Publishers.

THE NIGHT ABRAHAM CALLED TO THE STARS. Copyright © 2001 by Robert Bly. All rights reserved. Printed in the United States of America. No part of this book may be used or reproduced in any manner whatsoever without written permission except in the case of brief quotations embodied in critical articles and reviews. For information address HarperCollins Publishers Inc., 10 East 53rd Street, New York, NY 10022.

HarperCollins books may be purchased for educational, business, or sales promotional use. For information please write: Special Markets Department, HarperCollins Publishers Inc., 10 East 53rd Street, New York, NY 10022.

First Perennial edition published 2002.

*Designed by David Lane*

Library of Congress Cataloging-in-Publication Data is available.

ISBN 0-06-093444-1

02 03 04 05 06 ❖/RRD 10 9 8 7 6 5 4 3 2 1

*For Dr. Nurbahksh*

# ACKNOWLEDGMENTS

I'm grateful to the editors of the following magazines, in whose pages some of these poems first appeared:

*The New Republic, The Nation, Lapis, Literary Imagination, American Poetry Review, Paris Review, Agni, Atlantic Monthly, The Bitter Oleander, Sewanee Review, Southern Review, The Kenyon Review, The Partisan Review, Five Points, Poetry-Bay, Luna, The Reading Room, Raritan, Times Literary Supplement, Stand, PEN.*

"The Night Abraham Called to the Stars," "What Kept Horace Alive," "Iseult and the Badger," and "Why Is It the Spark's Fault?" originally appeared in *Poetry*.

# CONTENTS

# PART ONE

# The Night Abraham Called
## to the Stars

Do you remember the night Abraham first called
To the stars? He cried to Saturn: "You are my Lord!"
How happy he was! When he saw the Dawn Star,

He cried, "You are my Lord!" How destroyed he was
When he watched them set. Friends, he is like us:
We take as our Lord the stars that go down.

We are faithful companions to the unfaithful stars.
We are diggers, like badgers; we love to feel
The dirt flying out from behind our hind claws.

And no one can convince us that mud is not
Beautiful. It is our badger soul that thinks so.
We are ready to spend the rest of our life

Walking with muddy shoes in the wet fields.
We resemble exiles in the kingdom of the serpent.
We stand in the onion fields looking up at the night.

My heart is a calm potato by day, and a weeping,
Abandoned woman by night. Friend, tell me what to do,
Since I am a man in love with the setting stars.

# The Wildebeest

Once more the murky world is becoming confused. Oh
The essence of Reason's House *is* confusion,
So this development is like the owl becoming owlish.

Arithmetic has failed to bring order to our sorrow.
Newton is not guilty, because the man who
Invents the knife is not responsible for the murder.

Bees, abandoned by their Queen, clump
Together in the dusty light of the hemlocks.
Even programmers don't know when she will return.

The Herd Girl and the Shepherd Boy spend all year
At the opposite shores of the Milky Way.
In spring the lovers receive one night together.

The wildebeest leaps into the river spread-legged
Among the crocodiles; and the wolf packs are sad
Chasing the caribou endlessly over the steppes.

The beaver make their dens over and over, Grandmother
After grandmother dies, and nothing changes.
The Moses of the beaver does not see the Promised Land.

# Jerez at Easter

Please tell me why the lamb is in love with the wolf
And why the child's finger calls the hammer down
And why at dusk Alexander walks toward his enemies.

Tell me why the gazelle grazes so close to the lion
And why the rat makes up games on the snake's tail
And why the student bends his head when he's attacked.

One meadow in the redwoods can contain a thousand ferns.
By this we deduce we are living in the serpent's home.
Each curly fern is his tongue unfolding.

The poet makes a meadow from each leaf.
Each curve of language turns into a lamb's ear,
Because a genius is a child in the house of suffering.

None of us is free from a certain bend in the knee.
The caws from the oak-bound ravens in the trees
Around our house guide Alexander toward the night.

The old man's voice breaks as he sings at Easter.
In between the clapping, there's always a voice breaking.
Last night in Jerez some people lived, some people died.

# Giordano Bruno and the
## Muddy Footprint

Furry demons come to the door offering separations.
The crane's foot in the mud is the map of our life.
That sucking sound of the farm boot is the planet's cry.

Curly hair guards the opening to the womb.
Because there is heaven inside the womb, we will not allow
Our eyes to turn away from a single black hair.

There is so much glory in the great hooves
Of the stag that Tristan tracks through the glen,
And so much fear in the naked footprint near the river.

It's all right to praise the raven's dark feet,
And the crows settling down at dusk in the oak,
For setting stars always predict the stars that rise.

The web in the morning speaks of the origin of all dew.
The lovers look at each others' bodies so carefully,
And they need no more, and see all India there.

What relaxes us comes from God. It was when
He first saw the print of the sparrow's foot in the mud
That Giordano Bruno knew that the world was on fire.

# Moses' Cradle

The Pharaoh's wives touch the mud with their toes.
You and I float in Moses' cradle. Dear friends, you and I
Are parted by a thin skin from the ignorance of the Nile.

Ghosts compose themselves from ground mist.
Friends, our souls are moist. "Dry souls are best."
Plotinus thought so, but he was nursing at eleven.

Some children hear the thin words spoken by the dead.
Men piece out secrets hidden in prime numbers.
Women report what Eternity has told them to say.

Our cradle, like Moses', is porous to the Nile.
You and I will never have one whole day of light.
At three o'clock, a wall will creak, or a hare will die.

Beauty has reached us drenched in birth blood.
As our eyes open, bright blood splashes on the floor.
The baby's descent gives us a taste for war.

Some souls remember well, climb so high
They are remembered forever. But Macbeth fell
A thousand miles when the feathers touched his face.

# The Dead of Shiloh

"A drowsy numbness pains my sense." Keats heard
The nightingale cry out from the place of war.
He heard the thud of the buffalo-killer's gun.

The slant soul loves to play cards in the serpent's house.
The crow arrived only yesterday on Noah's boat
With the mud of Abraham's earth between his toes.

Shiloh was like a drug that hid secretly
Among the rough leaves on the Natchez Trace.
All the drinkers wanted it, and fell asleep.

We value addition and subtraction too much.
Ten thousand Newtons wrapping their equations
Around the serpent's tail can't replace a single lover.

The sunfish flashes light to the reeds below.
Moonlight slips inside the oyster's closed eyes.
The Light of Heaven widens the frog's mouth.

We float in the shadows below the dock.
But a dark hook hangs farther down.
There is nothing on that hook but "Farewell."

# When We Became Lovers

Do you laugh or cry when you hear the poet sing?
"Out of the first warmth of the spring, and out
Of the shine of the hemlocks . . ." It's the hemlocks then,

Swaying above the grasses in the cemetery,
That encourage us in our affair with the world.
We have secret meetings with moss at night.

When the night-singer sang, did you notice the mice
Going by? They leave tracks like the setting stars.
Haven't you heard the grunting of the hollyhocks,

Bringing forth their hairy life by the widow's door?
Gravestones gather up the stray tufts of time
That wind would otherwise scatter in the fields.

You and I have been in love with the moon
Rising for a long time, ever since the day
Our mothers took our hands in the spring field.

That was the day we heard the cry of the hemlocks.
We became lovers then; and our road was decided.
We laughed and cried over the warmth of the spring.

# Monet's Haystacks

It's strange that our love of Beauty should lead us to hell.
I caught one glimpse of you, and a moment later
My house and books were all thrown into the fire.

Plato wrote by the light from sharks' teeth.
There is always terror near the Quiet Garden.
If we have come to a bad end, let's blame Beauty.

The horses of sorrow are always restless, breaking
Out of fences, trampling the neighbors' garden.
The best odes are written by pirates in the moonlight.

When Monet glimpsed the haystack shining in fall dawn,
Knowing that despair and reason live in the same house,
He cried out: "I have loved God!" And he had.

I walked down the aisles of the grocery, weeping.
Gleams of light came off my hair when I saw you,
And I found myself instantly under the horses' hooves.

My improvidence was to have been too hopeful.
My improvidence was not to see the fall.
I apologize to those in hell for my disturbances.

# What Kept Horace Alive

Men and women spend only a moment in Paradise.
The two lovers watch Charlie Chaplin eat his shoe,
And a moment later find themselves barefooted in the grave.

I know that I wanted more than two years with you.
If my wife had been able to absorb more cruelty,
Perhaps I could have paid the fiery angels to go away.

The dead man lies in bed with his great toe
Sticking up; it is because of his toe
That he could carry the burden of marriage so long.

Sometimes I frighten that boy who sleeps on the ground.
He keeps his head in his arms; all he smells is the hair
That is left behind when the groundhog is eaten.

There are as many groundhogs as there are stars.
Wherever there is a lot of anything, we are in trouble.
It is the generosity of snowflakes that leads us to suicide.

The bats' wings are the Saviours of the mosquitoes;
And the cod long for the net. It was only the certainty
Of death that kept Horace alive so long.

# The Love from Far Away

We have a longing for the mud on riverbanks,
And for the wet earth around growing carrots.
When Jaufre Rudel spoke of the love from far away,

He was already bathing his head in lion's blood.
He wasn't that crazy about freedom! He cried out,
"I want to be held prisoner by the Arabs!"

The mourning dove is so well named; its brief call
Rises out of Eternity on a thin ash branch;
And the mother reaches for her son in the silence.

The moment the dove caught one glimpse of the Face,
The hollyhocks rooted themselves in the ground.
Only rooted oysters are able to produce pearls.

Swimmers, when they dive to the pool-floor,
Turn sometimes and look up toward the sky;
They see sunlight killing its bulls in the water.

"Cry out when your feet touch the bottom! We'll
Follow the bubbles down to where you are." Even
Underwater we can hear the mourning dove.

# PART TWO

# Eudalia and Plato

The Dutch have been growing tulips since 1500.
There are eight thousand tulips in one Dutch field.
Every century is full of lovers; so it's not to worry.

Clouds drift over the sea when the wind blows.
Dickens knew there are lovers even in the Law Courts—
The lovers without lawyers receive vast settlements.

The lovers' books are always open to Inspection.
We can see Romeo and Juliet in the tomb,
And paintings of tiny ships in Divine Waters.

Always the lover's body is saving and spending.
During the day its donkey gathers thousands of pearls.
Then at night it spends all that the earth has saved.

Eudalia will not allow Plato to come near
The Garden of Lovers because Eudalia knows
He, being lofty, is afraid of the glory of ruin.

I know how much ruin love can bring.
But at night I hang around the orchard
Hoping to catch one breath from the lovers' tree.

# The Trap-Door

Men and women spend only a moment in Paradise.
Then a trap-door sends them down to the Lords of
    Misreason,
Where baby kangaroos carry us all off in their small
    pouches.

Let's all praise the saints who never mention God!
Why should the Leghorn family praise the Knife-Grinder?
I don't think it's right for water to assist the grindstone,
    either.

The walls of my poetry house are splashed with blood.
I don't want to be inward. Every day a thousand mice
Run out my door heading for Tennyson's house.

Arabs with big eyes studied all night for years
And translated the Tablets of the Alchemists.
They could pull Mercury from the knees of the wind.

Jabir the Brilliant at fourteen could arrange
Sounds so they became holy. Friends, each day
I crawl over and kiss some of the books I love.

It is because the lovers have been exiled
To the nonexistence of the onion fields
That the pauper wakes up playing the flute of gratitude.

# Hannibal and Robespierre

We saw new ice in the ruts on the way to school.
Once I saw through the ice, even dying sheep
Could not convince me that the world is not right.

Sometimes ears of corn were left hanging
On the stalks. The picker had missed them. Those ears
Lay touching the ground the whole winter.

The dove's drunken call rising from the orchard
Where the young lambs stood near their mothers
Convinced me to throw in my lot with the dust.

I hope you've stopped saying that people
Are bad and animals good. Bees have their hives.
Every old frog is a son of Robespierre.

Our joy was ruined anyway long ago
For the sake of order; the boy's and girl's Delight
Would still be bound even if Rousseau got his way.

Hannibal's elephants never got back to Africa.
We know that the world loses many things. But
Even wars don't mean that the world is wrong.

# Walking Backward

Friends, there is only one joy and hundreds of sorrows.
We live down here in the Abode of Smelly Bones
Near the widow's door, near Whitman's retarded brother.

Even though it's dawn on the rooftops, it's still night
Here, among cabbages and shoats, among
Glints from the wings of the mice-seeking owls.

Sometimes milk makes us afraid. Savanarola
Was uncomfortable in a strawberry patch,
And Aristotle was uneasy beside the generous sea.

Mother's milk is what frightened both
The Italians and the Greeks. A drop of milk
Creates a crown when it falls back into milk.

The Sumerians, pressing their stylus into wet clay,
Found their way to the sites of their great
White-walled cities by the smell of milk.

In our messy world, we all walk backward,
Each holding a potato that points to the grave.
The night of infidelity and longing goes on forever.

# Wanting to Steal Time

People are moving big milk cans around in
The storeroom, and I am there. Each day I move
Barrels full of nothing to a different spot.

I want to charge you for the rustmarks on my pants.
When greed comes by, I hitch a ride on the truck.
You'll see nothing but my backside for miles.

Every noon as the clock hands arrive at twelve,
I want to tie the two arms together,
And walk out of the bank carrying time in bags.

Don't bother to associate poets with saints
Or extraordinary beings. People like us have already
Hired someone to weep for our parents.

We have a taste for ignorance, and a fondness
For the mediocre dressed up as fame. We love
To go with Gogol looking for dead souls.

Counting up the twelve syllables in a line
Could make us allies of the stern Egyptians
Whose armies were swallowed by the Red Sea.

# Calderón

Each mole and shoat is a shadow thrown by the sun.
Each muskrat, each badger, each hedgehog is a shadow.
That's why they can hide so well in the leaves.

Don't comfort me by putting flowers in my room.
Don't quote me the secret poems of Calderón.
Don't mention freedom in the execution room.

Each day I awake, the Lord of Greed senses
A new way to put my head down on the desk.
At a wedding I envy even the minister.

Whichever room I am in, he wants me to be
First, and I agree. So many injustices
Have come into the world through me.

The burning of monasteries is built into
Our world. In every great city you'll find
A Roman general living near Lucretia's house.

There are so many different designs of the snowflake.
There are so many halibut caught in the net.
There are so many salmon tails touching in the dark.

# The Wagon and the Cliff

The pin fails, and the wagon goes over the cliff.
The doctor steps out a moment and the boy dies.
We might question Emerson about this moment.

Please don't imagine that only people are greedy.
When a crow lifts off, its ungainly wings
Can carry a thousand Mandelas to the Island.

Hippolytus resisted women a little too much
And the Lady of the Sea decided against him.
His horses agreed to drag him along the stones.

Mourning doves singing from the fence posts
When I was a boy woke the whole countryside.
But a dove's breastbone is a cathedral of desire.

Sometimes the saints make us seem better than we are.
Our ancestors, on their passport photos, knew
The sound of a bird being pushed out of its nest.

Because I've become accustomed to failure,
Some smoke of sadness blows off these poems.
These poems are windows blown open by winter wind.

# Forgiving the Mailman

Let's celebrate another day lost to Eternity.
Minute by minute we eke out the story.
But the spider is on his way from night to night.

The mailman is not the one who ruins our life.
Wind has an affair with a million grains of sand.
Each sand grain has more power than Xerxes.

During those months while we slept in the womb,
The Demiurge gave us a taste for war
So that we were born mortgaged and howling.

Madame Bovary could not endure the good life.
She was like us: She wanted disgraceful nights,
Torn clothes, and the inconstant heart.

Our impoverishment follows naturally from our wealth.
The pain that man and wife feel at breakfast
Each day goes back to decisions in Heaven.

What will you say to Mahler about his daughter
Who died young? There were closed carriages in Vienna.
Freud tried to cure the insufficiency of our sorrow.

# The Way the Parrot Learns

I'm afraid to talk to you about my little toe,
Because I know that it will never agree to fasting.
The only ally I have is the sole of my foot.

We all live close to our greedy souls.
We have inherited so many longings
That in the other world our name is "So Many."

One teaspoon of envy was enough for me
To attack Robert Lowell; with a tablespoon
I could have taken on Henry James and Abelard.

Trainers once placed a parrot before a mirror,
And a man behind. The parrot, assuming
A parrot was speaking, would learn to talk.

Perhaps if God would put up a mirror
And sit behind it, and talk, I could believe
That those words of mercy were coming from me.

Why should the rooster go over every detail
Of his beheading? Let's leave some darkness
Around those days when danced in the road.

# Rembrandt's Portrait of Titus
## with a Red Hat

It's enough for light to fall on one half of a face.
Let the other half belong to the restful shadow,
The shadow the bowl of bread throws on the altar.

Some paintings are like a horse's eating place
At the back of the barn where a single beam
Of light comes down from a crack in the ceiling.

Painting bright colors may lie about the world.
Too many windows cause the artist to hide.
Too many well-lit necks call for the axe.

Beneath his red hat, Titus's eyes hint to us
How puzzled he is by the sweetness of the world—
The way the dragonfly hurries to its death.

So many forces want to kill the young
Male who has been blessed. The Holy Family
Has to hide many times on the way to Egypt.

Titus receives a scattering of darkness.
He's baptized by water soaked in onions;
The father protects his son by washing him in the night.

# PART THREE

# Nikos and His Donkey

Let's tell the sweet story about the day Nikos,
Wandering around with his donkey and saddlebags,
Turned up one day at a farm of Godseekers.

The Godseekers all came out when he knocked.
They welcomed him, gave him tea, brought
His donkey to the stable for oats and water.

"Stay for supper," they said. How glad he was!
They drank tea for hours. Dinner came.
They all ate happily and began to dance.

The Godseekers sang two lines over and over:
"Compared to God's, our song is only a bray;
How beautiful is the scent of a thousand hairs!"

In the morning, he said, "Could I have my donkey?"
They said: "What do you mean, your donkey?
You ate the meal! You danced. You sang the songs!"

The donkey we have loved for years may be killed
And cooked one day while we go on singing.
So don't write a single poem without gratitude.

# Pitzeem and the Mare

Let's tell the other story about Pitzeem and his horse.
When the One He Loved moved to the mountains,
He bought a mare and a saddle and started out.

He rode all day with fire coming out of his ears,
And all night. When the reins fell, the mare knew it right
Away. She turned and headed straight for the barn.

No one had told Pitzeem, but his horse had left
A new foal back in the stable. She thought of nothing
All day but his sweet face with its long nose.

Pitzeem! Pitzeem! How much time you've lost!
He put the mountain between the mare's ears again.
He slapped his own face; he was a good lover.

And every night he fell asleep once more. Friends,
Our desire to reach our true wife is great,
But the mare's love for her child is also great. Please

Understand this. The journey was a three-day trip,
But it took Pitzeem thirty years. You and I have been
Riding for years, but we're still only a day from home.

# The Country Roads

Last night in my dream, I drank tea steeped
In iron that had failed; at the bottom
I saw ruined tines of an old pitchfork.

Everything we leave behind is testimony,
Even our nail-clippings. Then my old clothes
Are testimony of my love of nakedness.

During the months everyone spoke badly of us,
Then I had the fiercest love for you.
People still try to encourage us by speaking badly.

So many times this week I've felt like weeping.
It's natural, like the cry of Canada Geese
Who call to each other over the darkening reeds.

In my early poems I praised so many lost things.
The way the crickets' cries in October carried
Them into the night sky felt right to me.

Every way of knowing is blessed by bootleggers.
Because the government does not allow delight
To be sold, you have to find it on the country roads.

# Iseult and the Badger

The ink we write with seeps in through our fingers.
What we call reason is the way the parasite
Learns to live in the saint's intestinal tract.

Even the finest reason still contains the darkness
From feathers packed together; General Patton
Was a salmon who grew large in the Etruscan pool.

All our language is woven from animal hair.
The badgers and the thrushes soak up the stain of
     separation,
Just as lanolin makes the shearer's hands soft.

The old thinkers of quiddity remind us
Of the fear the hogs feel hanging by their hind legs;
For we know our throats are open to the unfaithful.

"I was climbing on the sounds of my lover's
Name toward God," Iseult said. "Then a badger ran past.
When I said, 'Oh badger,' I fell to earth."

Perhaps if we used no words at all in poems
We could continue to climb, but things seep in.
We are porous to the piled leaves on the ground.

# In Praise of Scholars

Furry shadows are bringing gifts to our door.
We have nowhere to live but with the moles.
We'll have to pay the mortgage on the house of sorrow.

Our house is roofed with the shingles of parting.
Children there slide off their mothers' knees;
The door leads inward to silent wives and husbands.

My father wrote numbers down all his life
With a short, blunt pencil. Even Aristotle
Found himself caught in his dark reason.

It's too late to move now, friends. We'll have to pay
For years—yes!—and the interest rate is fixed.
It will require our lives, as it did our parents'.

Hundreds of scholars work in the basement.
They are good students of the ten thousand things.
Without them we would be at war forever.

There is only one mortgage and so many forms of payment!
There is one peace and so many forms of war.
The furry shadows are bringing gifts to the door.

# The Fish in the Window

"The fish are in the fishman's window," the grain
Is in the hall, "the hunter shouts as the pheasant falls."
That shout rises from deep in Adam's chest.

The great trawlers pull in the shining bodies.
Horses' teeth rip night from sleepy day.
We are all like Nebuchadnezzar on his knees.

Because the greedy soul gained its teeth in the womb,
More than one twin died in the safest place;
We fell into the doctor's hands with haunted eyes.

We inherited much when we inherited teeth.
We will never have one whole day of peace.
An old horse will die or a house will burn.

Each evening we reach for our neighbor's food.
Each night we crawl into imaginary beds;
Each midnight we visit the darkness with Saturn.

We can go on sitting in the Meeting House,
But the greedy one in us will still survive.
One cry from the crow contains a thousand more.

# Montserrat

Why God allowed Montserrat to fall
Is not explained, nor why the Queen of Cattle
Drove my one calf into the slaughterhouse.

My poems are sad. How could it be otherwise?
The judge and the criminal live in my own house.
I come constantly upon secret court proceedings.

Why do we achieve organization only in wartime?
I want to know why so many plays of Sophocles were lost,
And why God becomes an ox and eats the grass each night.

When I was twenty-six, I sent the words that fed me
To be killed, along with vowels that joined me to others;
My calf of language was cut up and thrown into the ditch.

My small talent was weighted down beneath the water,
And the lungs I breathed with were filled with lies.
If I had been human, it would have been worse.

That is what separation is like: I know it now.
I had only will to save me from drowning.
I was unfaithful even to Infidelity.

# The French Generals

Whenever Jesus appears at the murky well,
I am there with my five hundred husbands.
It takes Jesus all day to mention their names.

The growing soul longs for mastery, but
The small men inside pull it into misery.
It is the nature of shame to have many children.

Earth's name is "Abundance of Desires." The serpent
Sends out his split tongue and waves it
In the air scented with many dark Napoleons.

The general ends his life in a small cottage
With damp sheets and useless French franc notes;
He keeps his old plans of attack under the mattress.

I say to the serpent: "This is your house."
I bring in newspapers to make his nest cozy.
It's the nature of wanting to have many wives.

So many rafters in life jackets are pulled down
Till their toes touch the bottom of the Rogue River.
Wherever there is water there is someone drowning.

# The Battle at Ypres, 1915

Tammuz, bright with feathers, goes to the Underworld.
The peat-bog man sleeps on his slanted face.
Not to worry; it means that spring has come.

Naked men crawl into tunnels to retrieve the giant
Snakes. They don't resist if pulled out backwards.
Ah, friends, the world pulls us out backwards.

Some say that every bit of iron we pull
Out of the earth, and shape, we have to pay for.
At Ypres we paid dearly for the Bentley car.

Some greedy part hankers for disaster, for things
To go wrong, for the war to start. Many people
Are disappointed when the bombing is canceled.

Events at times turn out exactly wrong with us.
The Magi are misled by a satellite in the night;
And a rabbit sacrifices people during our Easter.

How happy the Europeans were in 1914!
It seemed as though spring had come at last!
Our gaiety the morning of war is momentary.

*For Martín Prechtel*

# The Raft of Green Logs

Poetry is an occupation appropriate for slaughterers
And knife-wielders. Life on earth needs many kills
To engender the soft leaps of the cheetah.

God made me tender; but writing poetry,
With its furry herd of images that have
To be saved or murdered, has made me fierce.

The Lord of this World condemns half his friends
To death. Music testifies to that. Notes
Wave their arms and sink into the cold Atlantic.

During the years I called to Rilke and Boehme,
I hung on to small branches; I went over
The waterfall still holding the twig of reason.

It's all right if we tumble down the falls.
I remember how many lambs died on the farm.
Our desires reform themselves overnight anyway.

My affections were stuffed into the giant's mouth.
Some marriages are rafts. I saw water between
The green logs. You could not have saved me.

# PART FOUR

# The Five Inns

When I cry, I want everyone else to cry.
I wanted to live at the edge of things as a boy.
A thousand geese gawping were just right for me.

A thousand red-eyed dragons live in a drop
Of clear water, all guarding the same treasure.
A hundred Jesuses are walking near Emmaus.

What are the five inns of the Dark One?
Smoke, fire, wind, mud and darkness.
Each of these casinos is delicious to the gambler.

My greedy soul and I share the same room.
When I see a book written two thousand years
Ago, I check to see if my name is mentioned.

Men and women like me who put their trust
In the dusky footsteps of the setting stars
Have secret accomplices in the world of night.

Yesterday's Caribbean storm rose when a gnat
Lifted its wing; and there are hundreds of Platos
And Ibn Arabis teaching the pupil of the eye.

# The Baal Shem and Francis Bacon

"The Five Ways of Knowing the World" worries me.
The thrush has so many tiny feathers around its bill
That a thousand ways of knowing might be closer.

Some old souls living in the Divine House felt
Such fear at the amount of darkness God
Left inside man during the Second Creation,

That they hid themselves away in an inner room,
And so never looked down at those tall grasses
Where Adam sat killing rabbits by the first fire.

When the Baal Shem was about to be born,
His soul was chosen from among that group of souls
Who had turned their eyes away from the window.

That's why the Baal Shem could travel a hundred
Miles in two hours and arrive just in time
To give the poor daughter money for her marriage.

That's why Francis Bacon could never understand
How the world gives away her secrets, nor how
Joseph could rise up from the bottom of his well.

# Natchez Inns

Let's just stay here weeping over old grain.
We've spent hours asleep, and other hours,
Dozens of them, hitched to the black horse.

We love most those hours that carry the burnt flavor
Of the stars; but we have to have praised God
For hours before the burnt minute appears.

Whenever we set a foot down, it is caught.
The steps we take resemble those Natchez inns
Where each pillow covers an open knife.

The bird can sing for hours through its beak!
It picks its grain carefully. But we, the sons
Of forgetfulness, eat the flesh that died shouting.

We have to fight the Agent of Disappointment a year
To love one disappearing star for a moment, because
Any star may carry us close to Orion's belt.

Be frank with me: Tell me how many dead hours
You have eaten, whom you have killed
While waiting for the Lord of this planet to fall asleep.

# The Cabbages of Chekhov

Some gamblers abandon carefully built houses
In order to live near water. It's all right. One day
On the river is worth a thousand nights on land.

It is our attraction to ruin that saves us;
And disaster, friends, bring us health. Chekhov
Shocks the heavens with his dark cabbages.

William Blake knew that fierce old man,
Irritable, chained and majestic, who bends over
To measure with his calipers the ruin of the world.

It takes so little to make me happy tonight!
Four hours of singing will do it, if we remember
How much of our life is a ruin, and agree to that.

Butterflies spend all afternoon concentrating
On the buddleia bush; human beings take in
The fragrance of a thousand nights of ruin.

We planted fields of sorrow near the Tigris.
The Harvesters will come in at the end of time
And tell us that the crop of ruin has been great.

# The Eel in the Cave

Our veins are open to shadow, and our fingertips
Porous to murder. It's only the inattention
Of the prosecutors that lets us go to lunch.

Reading my old letters I notice a secret will.
It's as if another person had planned my life.
Even in the dark, someone is hitching the horses.

That doesn't mean I have done things well.
I have found so many ways to disgrace
Myself, and throw a dark cloth over my head.

Why is it our fault if we fall into desire?
The eel poking his head from his undersea cave
Entices the tiny soul falling out of Heaven.

So many invisible angels work to keep
Us from drowning; so many hands reach
Down to pull the swimmer from the water.

Even though the District Attorney keeps me
Well in mind, grace allows me sometimes
To slip into the Alhambra by night.

# Rembrandt's Etchings

The cross-hatching brings the night into the day,
Just as the donkey brings its cargo into Egypt.
I am a beggar reaching out my hand for darkness.

The cat can't explain how much the mouse loves
Its teaspoon of darkness; nor we why we sip
So thirstily from the pond made with a sharp stylus.

What is this? A monk and a girl in the corn?
He can no more keep his seed from rising
Than the kernel prevent the corn from coming up.

The resting hog is content, tied by one leg,
At least for now. She is far down on the earth;
And no longer remembers small boys or boiling water.

Joseph needs a lantern as he and Mary
Travel silently through the night. The donkey
Is about to put its hoof down in that darkness.

The hatching and shadowiness are everywhere.
The lion, standing by the pollarded willow,
Protects the old St. Jerome while he reads.

# The Cardinal's Cry

The cardinal's cry could be heard at Gettysburg.
Some stars have no choice but to set in the west.
It's always night in the grain-bin of birth.

Vintners made strong red wine from the battlefields
Where the Romans died; and we know that hundreds
Of mothers loved the buffalo killers' hands.

Every poem is a cover over something naked.
Emily Dickenson's poems are shawls woven
From the lengthened hair of the ignorant and insane.

Ducks are swimming in and out of the reeds
In the marshy lakes of the amygdala.
A hunter shoots at everything that flies by.

The tumbling of clowns is part of the abundance
That gives birth to death, along with bitter
Berries, charcoal and the first snow.

The muddler you are reading has lied to you
Often because he didn't want to see how many
Things cannot be saved even if Abraham returns.

# The Old St. Peter by Rembrandt

Noah's ship does not sail with its elephants forever.
The crying of the monkeys breaks off and starts again.
Even shame does not last a whole lifetime.

"It was dark," Peter said. "We were alone. We had
A single candle which shone on the steel breastplate
Of the Roman soldier. The whole town was asleep."

We are bubbles on the lips of our friends.
Each time they turn their heads, we drift toward the Pole;
We pass into the Many and return.

Who can say, "With God, the rest is nothing"?
Who can say, "I am a grandchild of the unfaithful"?
Who is able to wait one month to drink water?

We fell into weeping yesterday at five o'clock.
We wept because slavery has returned; we wept
Because the whole century has been a defeat.

Oh Peter! Peter! The night behind you is black.
A beam of light falls on your outworn face.
What can you do but lift up your hand for forgiveness?

*Chicago Museum of Art*

# Why Is It the Spark's Fault?

The soul is in love with marshy ground and snails,
With mud, darkness, wind, smoke and fire.
The cucumber and melon lead us back toward Heaven.

Why is it the spark's fault if the moment a hammer
Hits hot iron the spark curves toward earth?
In July even lightning cannot help itself.

Italian fiddlers are always ready to play
Near the enclosed bed of the Prodigal Son
While a plump woman cuts a pear with a small knife.

Let's keep disaster remembered in our poems.
Our memory feeds on ruin just as cows
Stand around drinking from river water.

Who stands for the melon? Seth, Abraham
And Shem. The lightness of grasshoppers suggests
They are taking in some fiddle music from the grass.

Please forgive me if I know so many words
And say so little. The Word catches in my throat,
Because some force does not want me to follow Abraham.

# Augustine on His Ship

Each time we bring a violin near the Nile River,
The low G string cries; it's like the cry a ribbon
Makes when a raven carries it into his nest.

No one knows what the jaguar's whisker feels
Immersed in the bathwater of St. Francis.
We each have to be careful talking of our betters.

How can the literalists with their heavy voices
Speak through the thin bill of the thrush, or the spark,
Alone in wet cow dung, call to its friends?

So much flesh muffles the slow bones
Of the beaver that it's difficult for light
To pass from the tip of the tail to the skull.

Perhaps that's why Rimbaud, whose gold tooth
Was so delicately tuned to the Milky Way
Of language, could still die as a slave trader.

Every fall the Kraken comes up and brushes
With his Gnostic arms the hull of the ship
On whose planks Augustine walks at night.

# PART FIVE

# The Difficult Word

The oaks reluctantly let their leaves fall,
And hesitatingly allow their branches to be bare;
And the bear spends all winter in separation.

The beauty of marriage is such that it dissolves
All earlier unions, and leads man and wife
To walk together on the road of separation.

It's a difficult word. The thought frightens us
That this planet with all its darkening geese
Was created not for union but for separation.

Suppose there were a dragon curled inside each drop
Of water, defending its gold. It's possible
That abundance has the same effect as separation.

We all knew nothing of this when we floated
In the joy of the womb; but when our lips touched
Our mother's breast, we said, "This is separation."

It is my longing to smooth the feathers
Of brown birds, and to touch the sides of horses
That has led me to spend my life in separation.

# Testifying to the Night

Perhaps the turtle loves his sturdy back too much.
So much happens when no one is watching.
Our hopes for the universe did not include last night.

Last week I met her again. In my dream I
Took a room in a German inn; and she was
There. No one else knew about it that night.

When the Queen of Hearts shows up, we throw
The rest of the cards down, and stand up.
We know that the game is over for that night.

We won't have to worry about waking each other
Up at dawn. And we won't bother about sleep.
Good ants carry us around the room all night.

When she comes, why not bet everything?
Sometimes we bet and we lose; and the dealer
Goes away with our head that night.

When one sings, it's best to light candles
All around the singers' feet. The candle is not lit
To give light, but to testify to the night.

# The Storyteller's Way

It's because the storytellers have been so faithful
That all these tales of infidelity come to light.
It's the job of the faithful to evoke the unfaithful.

Our task is to eat sand, our task is to be sad,
Our task is to cook ashes, our task is to die.
The grasshopper's way is the way of the faithful.

Even though you are a literalist, accept
The invitation to go to Pluto's wedding.
Haven't you learned yet that the stars are faithful?

For every planet, there are a million jellyfish
Shooting along who don't know night from morning.
So is the sea full of the unfaithful or the faithful?

A storyteller has to remember every turn
Of language so that we all know the moment
When the King decides to betray the faithful.

Every story I tell reveals how many tokens
Of loyalty I have forgotten, how often
I have exchanged places with the unfaithful.

*For Gioia Timpanelli*

# How This Wealth Came to Be

It's hard to know how all this wealth came to be.
Ishmael was not created from a fight with a whale.
The ocean is not wild enough to have created Melville's
    soul.

The hungry one in us did not come from seed.
Our old enemy is one of Adam's grandfathers.
He stood around looking at the shadow of the first soul.

The Ark landed on Ararat; but all those
Who came off the Ark know that the voyage
Was not long enough to produce Abraham's soul.

Oaks once darkened almost all of Great Britain,
Covering it with leaves. But squirrels rummaging
In a million acorns could not find Chaucer's soul.

How many boulders had to be ground down
To produce one square inch of the Sahara!
Maybe the moon gave birth to Mandela's soul.

There is a mystery about the birth of Jesus. All that
Snow that fell to earth Christmas Eve finally
Did shift for an instant the weight of Rome's soul.

# Noah Watching the Rain

I never understood that abundance leads to war,
Nor that manyness is gasoline on the fire.
I never knew that the horseshoe longs for night.

During my twenties I worked in the opal mines.
No one could open the door to Saturn's house.
I had no choice but to live in my father's night.

I am still a mouse nibbling the chocolate of sadness.
I am an Albigensian reading Bulgarian script.
I am a boy walking across England by night.

Each time we fold in the fingers of our left hand
We bring our ancestors close to each other, so they
Can lie on top of each other in the bed at night.

Soon our grandfather and grandmother will kiss
Once more. Then death will come in his Jewish hat,
And tell Noah to start praising the rainy night.

Even though I know that whenever I say the word
"Abundance," I am laying up trouble for ourselves,
I have no other way to express my love for the night.

# Listening

The goose cries, and there is no way to save her.
So many cheeps come from the nest by the river.
If God doesn't listen, why are we listening?

Very deep water covers most of the globe.
Whenever I see it, I think of St. John.
There is no remedy for deep water but listening.

The King and Queen already know about love;
They search for each other through the whole deck.
While we play our hands, they are listening.

The day we die, we'll each be like the fish
Abruptly jerked out of the water.
For him, it is the end of all listening.

Like thousands of others, I'm eating beet soup
In some Russian inn. People write letters
To me from heaven, but I'm not listening.

The hermit said: "Because the world is mad,
The only way through the world is to learn
The arts and double the madness. Are you listening?"

# So Be It. Amen.

There are people who don't want Kierkegaard to be
A humpback, and they're looking for a wife for Cézanne.
It's hard for them to say, "So be it. Amen."

When a dead dog turned up on the road, the disciples
Held their noses. Jesus walked over and said:
"What beautiful teeth!" It's a way to say "Amen."

If a young boy leaps over seven hurdles in a row,
And an instant later is an old man reaching for his cane,
To the swiftness of it all we have to say "Amen."

We always want to intervene when we hear
That the badger is marrying the wrong person,
But the best thing to say at a wedding is "Amen."

The grapes of our ruin were planted centuries
Before Caedmon ever praised the Milky Way.
"Praise God," "Damn God" are all synonyms for "Amen."

Women in Crete loved the young men, but when
"The Son of the Deep Waters" dies in the bath,
And they show the rose-colored water, Mary says "Amen."

# Dawn

Some love to watch the sea bushes appearing at dawn,
To see night fall from the goose wings, and to hear
The conversations the night sea has with the dawn.

If we can't find Heaven, there are always blue jays.
Now you know why I spent my twenties crying.
Cries are required from those who wake disturbed at dawn.

Adam was called in to name the Red-Winged
Blackbirds, the Diamond Rattlers and the Ring-Tailed
Raccoons washing God in the streams at dawn.

Centuries later, the Mesopotamian gods,
All curls and ears, showed up; behind them the Generals
With their blue-coated sons who will die at dawn.

Those grasshopper-eating hermits were so good
To stay all day in the cave; but it is also sweet
To see the fence posts gradually appear at dawn.

People in love with the setting stars are right
To adore the baby who smells of the stable, but we know
That even the setting stars will disappear at dawn.